Jesus, the New Adam

Jesus, the New Adam

Humanity's Steadfast Hope

Dennis J. Billy, CSsR

WIPF & STOCK · Eugene, Oregon

JESUS, THE NEW ADAM
Humanity's Steadfast Hope

Wipf & Stock
An Imprint of Wipf and Stock Publishers
199 W. 8th Ave., Suite 3
Eugene, OR 97401

www.wipfandstock.com

PAPERBACK ISBN: 978-1-5326-3864-0
HARDCOVER ISBN: 978-1-5326-3865-7
EBOOK ISBN: 978-1-5326-3866-4

Manufactured in the U.S.A.

In honor of
Jesus, the New Adam

"See, I am making all things new."

Rev 21:5

Contents

Introduction

CHRISTIANITY TELLS THE STORY of humanity's creation, fall, and redemption. It begins with the premise that the entire universe is a creation of a loving and benevolent God. It asserts that, at the dawn of time, man upset the order of the cosmos by overstepping his bounds and placing *himself* rather than *God* at the center of existence. Since all things are connected, and since humanity represents both the height of creation and its evolving self-awareness, this act of radical self-centeredness had serious consequences not only for humanity, but also for the whole of creation. The Christian narrative outlines the extent to which God would go to make things right. It says that he did so through the incarnation, passion, death, resurrection, and ascension of Jesus Christ.

Creation. Fall. Redemption. These mysteries form the backdrop against which our human story unfolds. To be properly understood, they must not be treated in isolation, but in the light they cast upon each other. Otherwise, they can easily fall prey to misinterpretation, false ideas, and unnecessary distortions. Taken alone, each captures only a part of the human story and runs the risk of losing its grasp of the whole. Taken together, they recount the narrative of humanity's origins, fall from grace, and ongoing re-creation. This completed narrative speaks to the human condition, addresses our deepest concerns, and has great relevance for our lives. It tells us that God entered our world in the person of Jesus Christ, gave himself to us completely, to the point of dying for us, in order to become nourishment and a source of endless hope for us.

It looks to Jesus Christ as the New Adam and affirms that his story has now become our own. It reminds us that those who believe in him have been immersed in his passion, death, and resurrection and have become members of his body.

Christians believe that Jesus is the Son of God, who entered our world to make all things new. His Incarnation affirms the two-fold mystery that humanity is capable of God (*capax Dei*) and, perhaps more importantly, that God is capable of man (*capax hominis*). His paschal mystery embodies the drama of how sin and death were overpowered by the wood of the cross and the Good News emanating from the empty tomb. His ascension into heaven points to the destiny we now share with him by virtue of the gift of faith and the outpouring of his Spirit upon his followers.

This book retells the narrative of Christ's redemptive journey. It does so by taking a hard look at some of the Gospel's underlying assumptions and showing how they are both reasonable and credible. For Christians, faith is not contrary to reason, but presupposes and even builds on it. This faith asks us to put aside whatever preconceptions we might have regarding the Gospel message and listen with an open heart to the way it speaks to the universal human condition. It invites us to consider this narrative in the light of its unique capacity to convey universal truths through concrete images. The story it tells is not a mere product of the human imagination, but reflects something within the mind of God himself. Since human beings reflect God's image and likeness, it follows that all that is good and noble in their minds somehow reflects the goodness and nobility of God himself. God writes his story, however, not with paper and ink, but on the pages of human history. The seed of hope buried deep within the mythologies of old is nothing but a faint reflection of God's dream for his creation. For Christians, this dream has entered the arena of history in the person of Jesus Christ, who sheds light on our human condition through his incarnation and paschal mystery. The presentation of the mysteries of creation, fall, and redemption in the pages that follow offers us a glimpse of our human destiny and how it is intimately bound up with Jesus, the New Adam, in the glory of the Risen Lord.

1

In the Beginning

CREATION AND FALL

> So God created humankind in his image,
> in the image of God he created them;
> male and female he created them. (Gen 1:27)[1]

THE CHRISTIAN MESSAGE MAKES little sense apart from the doctrines of creation and fall. These two beliefs are deeply Biblical and form the backdrop against which the narrative of redemption unfolds. Christianity both presupposes the Judaic foundations from which these doctrines come and builds on them. Without them, the story of our redemption has no narrative context or point of departure. The mysteries of the Incarnation and of Christ's passion, death, resurrection, and ascension exist because of the existence of creation and the reality of humanity's primal fall from grace. At the outset of our exploration of the mystery of redemption, it would do us well to take a close look at these two foundational Christian beliefs.

---

1. All quotations of Scripture come from *Holy Bible: New Revised Standard Version with Apocrypha* (New York: Oxford University Press, 1989).

Our Created World

The Bible begins with not one, but two accounts of creation (Gen 1:1—2:4; 2:5–25). This diversity indicates that we are dealing with a mystery that cannot be easily explained, and therefore needs multiple versions to deal with its elusive nature. These accounts are at the same time similar, yet different. The most obvious difference concerns the order of creation itself. In the first account, God creates humanity in his image, but does so at the end of his creative work; in the second, he creates humanity at the very outset from the dust of the earth and breathes into his nostrils the breath of life. Their similarity lies in the truths about the human condition they seek to convey. Together, they affirm both the goodness of creation and the unique status bestowed on humanity. They complement each other in a way that affirms the goodness of God and all he has made. They enable us to access certain truths concerning humanity's primal origins, and should therefore be read in light of one another. These truths cover a wide range of topics concerning human existence.

To begin with, the Christian belief in creation affirms the distinction between God and his creatures. This distinction lies at the very heart of the Christian message. For Christians, there can be no blurring of the boundaries between the natural and the supernatural. God is God, and creation is of his making. What God has made may bear certain similarities to him, but there can be no disputing the fact that what God has made is distinct from himself. Blurring this distinction, or simply doing away with it, elevates creation to the status of divinity and leads to pantheism, the view that gives divine status to everything that exists.

The Christian belief also affirms that God created the universe out of nothing. There was no primordial "stuff" from which God crafted his cosmos. To posit such a substance would lead to a metaphysical dualism, since it would recognize something other than God existing along side of him from all eternity. The term "nothing," moreover, should not be construed in such a way to be representative of this primordial "stuff," but as non-existence itself. The created world, when seen in this light, has its roots entirely in the mind of God and came into existence only at God's command.

The belief also teaches that the distance between the creator and his creation is so great that only God can bridge it. He does so by leaving traces or vestiges of himself in the created world and, in a special way, by implanting his image in the human soul. Even though the gap between the two is infinitely vast, God has chosen not to distance himself from his creation, but to reveal himself to us through the Law, the prophets, and ultimately through the incarnation of his Word. The doctrine, moreover, teaches that God is good and that his creation flows from his goodness. Action flows from being. To create something out of nothing involves an action that flows from the very being of God himself. For this reason, creation shares in God's being in varying degrees and thus participates in his goodness. The creation accounts affirm the fundamental goodness of all that God has made. Everything that exists—indeed, all of God's creation— possesses an intrinsic goodness that cannot be taken away from it. This "metaphysical" goodness must be distinguished from "moral" goodness, which depends not on existence itself, but on the free choice and the creature's personal decision to pursue good or evil.

Moreover, this belief maintains that God created the universe in such a way that parts of it have gained self-awareness, can inter-act freely with their environment, and relate to one another (and to God) in an intimate, personal way. Part of this freedom involves the ability either to enter into and sustain relationships, or to destroy them. God created the world so that it might enter into a meaning-ful and loving relationship with him. He created human beings to bear the weight of this responsibility by creating them in his image and bestowing upon them the powers of reason, memory, and will. God's image is also reflected in the complementarity of the sexes. Woman completes man, and man completes woman. The bond of love they share reflects the communal nature of God himself and affirms the Christian truth that "God is love" (1 John 4:8). The doctrine also asserts that God established a hierarchy in creation and placed humanity at its summit as its steward and caretaker.

God's creatures share in his being in varying degrees. While he has left a vestige of himself in all things, he has imprinted his image in all human beings. As stewards of God's creation, we have the responsibility to care for God's creatures and tend the garden of his creation so that it can reach its fullest potential. Humanity is both a part of creation and the steward responsible for it at the same time. God has entrusted us with great power over the created world, and we must answer for our actions accordingly.

Furthermore, because God is good, the belief does not attribute evil to God, but to creaturely free choice. Evil is parasitic in nature. It does not exist in and of itself, but represents a lack of something that ought to be there. This lack comes in the failure to recognize what is truly good, and to pursue instead what can only be described as a momentary, partial, and apparent good. God, in other words, does not cause evil, but merely permits it. He does so because he has endowed some of his creatures with the power of free will and fixed his eyes on the great good that could come from it. Although such a power naturally opens up the possibility of rejecting God's will in favor of our own, it also allows us to share in an intimate, loving relationship with him. God wants as many of these loving relationships as possible. Because he is a God of variety, he has given every person a unique voice, a fingerprint, a genetic blueprint, and much more, that makes him or her unique in all the world. In the midst of all this diversity, he has blessed humanity with an inherent love for unity. We are social beings capable of forming strong communal relationships. To live peaceably in community represents one of the primordial qualities and goals of human existence. Our capacity to do so is itself a reflection of the community within God himself.

These insights are but a few that flow from the Christian view of creation. They remind us that the teaching steers clear of pantheism and dualism, posits the goodness of God as the underlying foundation of existence, and envisions creation as a rich and highly diversified, multifaceted reality. They also identify a hierarchy within creation, place humanity at its summit, and charge it with its care. By virtue of being created in God's image, human beings are capable of entering into a loving relationship with God and reflecting that love in their own relationships. The love between man and woman reflects this love in a profound and very beautiful way. These insights represent the very best of God's providential plan for the universe and seem almost too good to be true. We need only take a good hard look at the world around us to see that things are not as they should be. The question arises for all of us: What went wrong?

Remembering the Fall

The Biblical account of the fall recounts the story of humanity's from grace (Gen 3:1–24). It relates how our earliest ancestors turned away from God to pursue their own selfish ends. It tells us how Adam and Eve ate from the tree of knowledge of good and evil, because they believed it would make them like God by giving them both the knowledge of and the power to decide what is good and what is evil. This sin was "original" not only because it came first, but also because it goes back to the very dawn of human existence. In this latter sense, it can also be referred to as the "sin of human origins."

Since the word "Adam" comes from the Hebrew word for "ground" and the word "Eve" from the Hebrew for "mother of all the living," the creation accounts refer to our original humanity and the turning away from God that occurred at the dawn of time and which had drastic effects for succeeding generations. These consequences are depicted in the subsequent chapters of Genesis (4—12), which describe the spread of sin sown from the seed of our ancestors that set humanity on a downward spiral of sin and corruption. The stories of Cain and Abel (Gen 4:1–26), Noah and the Flood (Gen 6:5—9:29), the Tower of Babel (Gen 11:1–32) and Sodom and Gomorrah (Gen 19:1–29) catalogue the destructive generational power of sin and its deep roots in the human soul. Since Adam and Eve also represent the summit of God's creation and its growing awareness of itself and its Maker, this sin of human origins had deep repercussions not only for humanity, but also for the whole of creation. This awareness was dimmed on account of our primeval fall from grace and the alienation that followed. Adam and Eve's expulsion from the garden of Eden symbolizes this darkened state (Gen 3:23–24). What is more, without its caretakers to tend and watch over it, creation itself would eventually sink into this deep, destructive mire. With paradise lost, humanity lost its access to the tree of life, wandered without purpose or direction, and was left to itself to toil under the pain of sin and death. The consequences of the fall continue to shape the human condition and affect our lives to this very day. Just what might these be?

To begin with, the sin of human origins caused humanity to take advantage of its role of stewardship and exploit creation for its own selfish gains. Humanity must be viewed as an integral part of creation with a unique role assigned to it by God. We represent creation coming to an awareness of itself, and we have been charged by God with the task of watching over and caring for his creation. The sin of our first parents had serious consequences, not only for human nature, which was seriously damaged by the action, but for the whole of creation, which suffered from the aftershock and ripple effects of this grave moral failure. When seen in this light, the sin of human origins is also the sin of creation's origins. It alienated humanity from the rest of creation and had grave human and environmental consequences from which we still suffer.

What is more, the anthropological consequences of the fall affected all levels of human experience: the physical, the mental, the spiritual, and the social. The sin of Adam and Eve had physical consequences, in the sense that they would now experience the pain of childbearing, the toil of labor, suffering due to disease and illness, and the reality of death. It had mental consequences in that it caused a darkening of the mind, a weakening of the will, and an unruly unleashing of the passions. It had spiritual consequences in that human beings no longer lived in communion with God, but were isolated from him and, as a result, also isolated from themselves, others, and the rest of creation. It had social consequences in that human consciousness sank from a communal self-awareness, which gave each individual a sense of responsibility for and belonging to the larger whole, to an exaggerated sense of individuality, which pitted persons against each other and the interests of the community. The sin of human origins was a historical event with transhistorical consequences. It occurred at the dawn of time, but had serious repercussions that haunt us to this very day.

As a result of humanity's primal fall from grace, creation itself grew out of sync with itself. Creation consists of a vast web of interconnected realities. It embraces all living and non-living things that depend on each other for their continuing sustenance and well-being. A change in any part of this web has a ripple effect throughout. As a result of the sin of human origins, creation has been left to itself. Like any untended garden, it has become unkempt and overgrown. It has become a dark and gloomy place of danger governed only by the principle of survival. With the sin of our first parents, creation has turned against itself, and humanity has become an instrument of its destruction rather than preservation. These ripple effects extend all along the entire spectrum of the created world, from the smallest subatomic particle to the immaterial world and the realm of the spiritual. All of creation has suffered from humanity's expulsion from the garden. Paradise has been lost and is in desperate need of being found.

As a result of humanity's primal fall from grace, human nature itself has become weakened and seriously flawed. The physical wounds of creation would soon become manifest in the body, as human beings began to experience the oppression of poverty, old age, disease, and ultimately death itself. These physical consequences, however, pale in comparison to the mental, spiritual, and social effects caused by the sin of our first parents. The darkening of the mind led to a weakening of our moral compass. The fire of truth and goodness which once blazed in the hearts of all human beings dimmed to nothing but a burning ember that could cast only faint light on the troubles of life. Our knowledge of the good lost its firm footing and devolved into a matter of personal taste and opinion. What is more, our wills became estranged from the will of God, weakening our ability to focus on the good, embrace it, and seek to implement it in our lives. Part of the reason for this is that our passions have become unruly as a result of the fall, and prevent our minds from seeing rightly and our wills from following through on its convictions.

Probably the most disconcerting (and most overlooked) consequence of the sin of human origins lies in the descent from collective to individual self-awareness. Before the fall, humanity was united by a collective spirit of unity and well-being. This communal awareness did not overwhelm the individual sense of self, but was primary in the minds of all who belonged to the human community. After the fall, however, this collective self-awareness became fragmented and out of sync with itself. The social fabric of the human community broke down into vying tribal affinities based on language, blood, and kinship. The story of the tower of Babel (Gen 11:1–9) describes this gradual breakdown of humanity's social fabric, as does any honest assessment of humanity's current situation in the world. Our present-day sense of solidarity and common good are but faint reflections of this prelapsarian state. We have forgotten that God relates to us, first as a people and only secondarily as individuals. This predilection on God's part for the collective over the singular points to this collective self-awareness that goes back the very dawn of our human origins. While the sin of the Adam disrupted this collective self-awareness, leaving behind nothing but faint traces in our collective memory, Christ—the New Adam—promises to restore in his glorified and risen body, the body of the church.

To this day, the ramifications of the fall continue to make their presence felt. The Christian view of reality hinges on the idea that something has gone awry in God's creation and that human beings are responsible for it. To deny this responsibility denigrates the important role humanity plays in the world's present and ongoing sustenance. Humanity must reclaim its role as the steward and caretaker of God's creation. Christians claim that it has done so in the person of Jesus Christ, the New Man, who has come to renew the world and make all things new.

Conclusion

The Christian doctrines of creation and fall convey some basic truths about the nature of existence and the role we play in it. These truths are couched in stories rich in symbolism and convey universal truths that are deeply relevant to our daily lives. These stories capture abstract truths in concrete form and present them in a way that resonates deep within our hearts. It is difficult to read the biblical accounts of creation without affirming the goodness of God and the work of his hands. It is also difficult to read the account of humanity's fall from grace without sensing that something has gone terribly wrong with God's creation and that the fault lies not with God, but with our very selves.

For Christians, these two teachings provide the backdrop for all that follows. They capture the essence of the human condition and form the opening acts of the drama of salvation history that begins with the patriarchs, continues in life of the Jewish people, and culminates in person of Jesus Christ. They are not ends in themselves, but a preparation for the redemptive action of Christ's paschal mystery and the appearance of the New Adam on the stage of human history. The doctrine of creation anticipates the new creation heralded by Christ and his preaching of the kingdom. The doctrine of the fall, in turn, looks to the restoration of humanity's hopes and dreams made possible by Christ's passion, death, and resurrection.

The stories of creation and fall are the opening acts of the drama of God's creative action, which brings into existence, sustains, and continues to make all things new. They contain within themselves the seed of all that follows. They carry us back to the dawn of our existence and help us to explore the origins of our world, the role we play in it, and the impact our choices have on our destiny. They help us to confront the truth about ourselves by asking us to savor the present moment as a manifestation of God's creative action, and to be aware of the temptation each of us faces to seize control of it rather than allowing it to unfold in due time. Most of all, they give us hope that the Good God, who created us and who keeps us in being, will not abandon us to ourselves, but reach out to us from across the heavens to help us find our way back to paradise.

Reflection Questions

- Do the doctrines of creation and fall supply the backdrop for the Christian narrative?
- What would Christianity look like without them?
- What truths do these doctrines seek to convey?
- What do they say about the world we live in?
- What do they say about us?
- What do they say about God?

Prayer

Lord, you made this world, and we have tarnished it.

Help us to get out of the way of your creative rebuilding.

2

He Dwelled Among Us

INCARNATION

> The angel said to her, "The Holy Spirit will come upon
> you, and the power of the Most High will overshadow
> you; therefore the child to be born will be holy; he will
> be called Son of God." (Luke 1:35)

GOD SHOWED US THE way back to paradise by entering our world
and becoming one of us. The mystery of the Incarnation affirms
the truth that a young Jewish woman from Nazareth conceived by
the power of the Holy Spirit and gave birth to a child, named Jesus, whose name means "God saves." As Catholics, we believe that
Jesus was the Son of God. He was, and is, the Word-made-flesh—
fully human, fully divine—like us in all things but sin. The Gospel
of Matthew calls him "Emmanuel, which means, 'God is with us'"
(Matt 1:23). The Gospel of John calls him "the way, and the truth,
and the life" (John 14:6). These titles are intimately related. Jesus,
we might say, is *God with us on the way*. He is the way, because he
is the truth and the life.

Jesus came into our world to show us the truth about ourselves. He came to show us what it means to be fully human. "For
the Son of God became man," Saint Athanasius says, "so that we
might become God."[1] "The glory of God," Saint Irenaeus tells us,

---

1. *Catechism of the Catholic Church*, no. 460.

"is man fully alive."[2] "The paradise of God," for Saint Alphonsus de Liguori, "is the heart of man."[3] These saints remind us that Jesus came to give us life, and to give it in abundance. He came not merely to save us, but to dwell within our hearts and befriend us. He tells his disciples in the Gospel of John, "I do not call you servants any longer . . . but I call you friends" (John 15:15). Jesus came to bring us plentiful Redemption—and that he did. In this chapter, we will explore the mystery of the Incarnation by looking at two basic questions: "How is it possible?" and "Why?"

How Is This Possible?

Difficulties arise when we entertain even the thought of God entering our world and becoming one of us. We wonder how is this possible. How could the divinity ever possibly enter the world of the finite? To many, the idea of God becoming human seems ludicrous, since the infinite and the finite simply do not mix. The mere thought of it makes one think of a children's story, something to dream about, but not anything that could ever actually happen. Many people think the entrance of the divine into the realm of the human is a pipe dream with no basis in reality.

Even in the early days of Christianity there were those who denied the reality of the Incarnation by saying that God did not actually become human, but merely appeared in human form. Others rejected it on the grounds that the material world was intrinsically evil and incapable of being a receptacle of the divine. The mystery of the Incarnation asks us to examine some of our most basic assumptions about what it means to be human. It involves the interplay of the ideas about the very nature of God, humanity, and the world. It asks us to entertain the possibility that an infinite, all-powerful, and loving God emptied himself of his divinity and entered the world he created to become fully human. Let us examine this possibility in more detail.

2. Ibid., no. 294.

3. de Liguori, *The Way to Converse Always*, 395.

Our Elusive God

Let us begin with the notion of God. At the very outset, it is important for us to state that the nature of God is elusive and will always remain a mystery to the human mind. Even though Christianity is based on the idea that God has revealed himself to us through the prophets of Israel and ultimately in the person of Jesus Christ, we must humbly admit that we know very little about him. Our finite minds cannot exhaust the meaning and nature of the infinite. The supernatural reveals only as much as the natural can contain at any given moment. There will always be something more for us to discover about the nature of the Godhead. This does not mean that what God has revealed is not true. It simply means that there is still much more for God to unveil, much more for him to reveal about himself.

Besides, what God has chosen to reveal to us is quite substantial in itself and requires time to ponder and digest. The Christian teaching that God is love (1 John 4:8) tells us something about the divine nature. We know from our own experience that authentic love is both social and self-diffusive. It reaches out to others in ways that are both life-giving and life-receptive. A truly loving person knows how to give the gift of self and receive it. Since authentic love must be oriented toward another, to say that God is Love implies the presence of both Personhood and Otherness within God. Since God's personhood goes beyond the boundaries of our limited experience, it might even be better to refer to him as "Suprapersonal." God's personhood, in other words, relates to our known experience of personhood in the same way the supernatural relates to the natural.

The Christian belief in the Trinity resolves the philosophical problem of the One and the Many by uniting them in the unfathomable mystery of Divine Love. It affirms both the fundamental oneness of God and the social fabric of his being. To say that there are three Persons in one God—Father, Son, and Holy Spirit—affirms the intimate connection between God and Love. The doctrine claims that, from all eternity, the Father has loved, loves, and will love the Son. And it says the same about the Son's love for the Father. The love that binds them, moreover, is itself the Person of the Holy Spirit. It is by the power of this Spirit that God created the universe. It is by this same power that a virgin conceived and bore a son in the mystery of the Incarnation.

God is not only love; he is also existence itself. He created the world and keeps it in being from one moment to the next. His act of creation is both continuous and ongoing. "Existence is *guttatim*," as the saying goes; it is bestowed "drop by drop." Things exist because God imparts existence to them from one moment to the next. The difference between them and God is that they receive existence and only share in it, while God *is* existence itself and only allows his creation to participate in it. This sharing in God's existence lies at the very heart of the mystery of the Incarnation. The infinite God can enter the finite world because its very existence comes from and is sustained by his love.

J. B. Phillips wrote a popular book called *Your God is Too Small.*[4] We can learn a great deal from this simple title, not the least of which is that we must not limit God to the narrow confines of what our petty imaginings have made him out to be. We need to break out of the false conceptions of God that blind us to the real possibilities before an all-powerful and all-loving God. These false images ("idols," if you will) prevent us from realizing that all things are possible for God, and this includes the possibility of entering our world and becoming one of us. These limiting ideas hold us back from recognizing that, in varying degrees, all of creation is "capable of God" (*capax Dei*) and that the human person, who exists at creation's height and has been shaped in God's own image, is especially so. Why is this so? The Christian response is that, because of free will, only we are capable of entering into relationship with him and love him in return.

4. Phillips, *Your God Is Too Small.*

Our Human Existence

Now let us turn to the notion of ourselves. The mystery of the Incarnation states that God entered our world and became one of us. According to the classical Christian doctrine, Jesus Christ is the Word made flesh, both fully God and fully human at the same time. Christians believe that Jesus is the God-man, the Second Person of the Blessed Trinity, who has both a human and a divine nature mystically joined in what as known as the hypostatic union. The appearance of Jesus on the stage of world history set in motion a process of reflection that ultimately led the church he established to come to a deeper understanding of both the divine and the human. This understanding steered clear of two extremes: one that emphasized Jesus' divinity to the exclusion of his humanity, and another that did just the opposite. By affirming Jesus' full divinity and full humanity, the mystery of the Incarnation opened up new avenues into our understanding of God, man, and the relationship between them.

Had it not been for Jesus, we probably never would have come to think of God as a Blessed Trinity of Father, Son, and Holy Spirit. Confronted with Jesus' message and the repercussions of his paschal mystery, the early church had to determine whether Jesus was divine or merely human. The Council of Nicea's solemn declaration that he was "from the substance of the Father"[5] opened the door to reflection on the nature of the Godhead that eventually led to the dogma of the Holy Trinity. Similarly, without Jesus we probably would not have come to understand what it means to be truly human. When we look at him, we see a man fully alive with the love of God. Everything about him radiated an intimacy with the divine that had never been seen before. Because of him, this intimacy is also offered to us. We look at him and recognize that we are all called to share in what the Son has freely received from the Father. The Father wishes to impart this love to us so that, like Jesus his Son, we too might become fully alive.

5. See Denzinger, *Enchiridion*, 50–51.

A key aspect of the mystery of the Incarnation is that God assumed all of our humanity and was like us in all things but sin. We are multidimensional creatures with physical, mental, spiritual, and communal aspects to our nature. The Apostle Paul touches on each of these dimensions in his letters. At one point he writes: "May the God of peace himself sanctify you entirely; and may your spirit and soul and body be kept sound and blameless at the coming of our Lord Jesus Christ" (1 Thess 5:23). To these spiritual, psychological, and physical dimensions he adds the social in his teaching on the body of Christ: "For just as the body is one and has many members, and all of the members of the body, though many, are one body, so it is with Christ" (1 Cor 12:12). When he became one of us, God entered into every dimension of our human existence and made them his own in a new and entirely different way. He took them to himself and, in doing so, purged them of all earthly blemish, illuminated them with the divine light, and thoroughly transformed them from the inside out. The mystery of the Incarnation demonstrates that God's plan for humanity was to divinize it by filling it with the light of divine grace.

In the church's reflection on the person of Jesus Christ—his identity, power, and purpose—theology and anthropology have become intimately connected. Meditating on Jesus forces us to ask questions about the very nature of God himself, and who we are as persons capable of relating to him. If Jesus is "the way, and the truth, and the life" (John 14:6), then he alone can show us the way to God and he alone can show us what it means to be truly human. The mystery of the Incarnation tells us that human destiny can no longer be separated from the person of Jesus Christ. His passion, death, resurrection, and ascension into heaven reveal to us a path that that we too must follow by virtue of our faith that turns us into members of his body.

Jesus once said, "If any want to become my followers, let them deny themselves and take up their cross and follow me" (Mark 8:34). As a result of his paschal mystery, Jesus' followers are mystically united to his glorified existence. We deny ourselves by embracing his narrative and allowing it to become our own. Following him means that, like him, we too must die to ourselves and embrace the Father's will for us. It means being willing to enter the world of those around us and to give ourselves to them so that we can become nourishment for them and a source of hope. Most of all, it means allowing Jesus to befriend us so that he can dwell in our hearts and we might dwell in his. It means being able to say with the Apostle Paul, "I have been crucified with Christ; and it is no longer I who live, but it is Christ who lives in me" (Gal 2:19–20).

The World We Live In

Finally, let us turn to the world around us. According to Christian belief, God created the universe and placed humanity at its pinnacle to care for it. This hierarchical view of the interplay among the three draws a clear distinction between God and his creatures, and also identifies a hierarchy within creation itself. The "hierarchy of being," as it is called, recognizes that the creatures made by God participate in existence in varying degrees. Thus man, who was created in God's image, shares in God's existence in a deeper manner than, let us say, a horse, or a tree, a blade of grass, or a stone.

This hierarchy, however, should not be understood in a sense of a struggle for survival, a will to power, or the domination of the strong over the weak. If such attitudes exist, they are more representative of the fallen world in which we live than of God's original purpose. In the Christian view of things, hierarchy is a fundamentally positive concept and is considered the way in which God brings order in the universe. Our role in the hierarchy of creation is not to take advantage of it by using it as we please, but to cultivate it so that its own inner beauty and purpose can shine forth. When viewed in this light, we are the servants of creation and have been delegated by God to watch over and care for it. Since we ourselves are creatures of God, our role as stewards of creation is actually a form of creation's self-cultivation. Through our care for the world, creation is actually tending itself. The poor job we are doing of it is not due to God's original intention, but to our primeval fall from grace which had internal repercussions on the human soul and external ones of the world without.

Recognizing our privileged place in the vast hierarchy of creation helps us to overcome some latent preconceptions many of us have about the world of matter. There is a tendency on the part of some to think of matter and spirit as two diametrically opposed principles vying with each other for dominance. Some seek to resolve this tendency by such philosophies as materialism and panpsychism: the former denies the existence of the spiritual world by somehow collapsing it into material; the latter, by way of contrast, states that all of existence (even the material) is fundamentally mental or spiritual in nature.

A more nuanced approach comes from Aristotelian philosophy as adapted by Thomas Aquinas, which states that the visible world represents a composite relationship of matter and form (the "hylomorphic theory," as it is called). In this view, matter cannot exist in the visible world without having some kind of shape or form. What this visible thing *is* depends on the intimate relationship between the two. Matter, by this reckoning, is intrinsically open to being shaped and thus receiving some kind of form. The nature of this form depends on where the thing is located along the hierarchy of being and the degree to which matter is capable of receiving the form. The form of a plant is a vegetable soul; that of an animal, an animal soul; that of a human being, a rational soul.

According to this scenario, matter in its primary, formless state is capable of being shaped and coexisting with the invisible realm of form. When applied to our current discussion, it is not an unworthy receptacle of the invisible, spiritual realm, since even in its fallen, corrupted state it possesses a fundamental nobility by virtue of its being God's own handiwork. Because it comes from God, matter is, by its very nature, capable of receiving at least some level of the spiritual. This insight makes the possibility of an infinite God entering the finite material world something within the capability of an all-powerful and all-loving God.

Conclusion

The mystery of the Incarnation causes us to reflect deeply about the nature of God, man, and the world. It challenges us to think outside the box and to examine some of our most basic assumptions about the nature of reality and the spectrum of possibility. It causes us to think of the extent to which an all-powerful and all-loving God would go in order to save us from ourselves and lead us away from our self-centeredness and back to the path of goodness and right. Because it is a mystery, we will never fully understand just how spirit and flesh, the infinite and the finite, the supernatural and the natural, would interact in God's becoming man. What we *do* know, however, is more than enough to say that it is, at the very least, something that makes sense to finite minds; something that is plausible and, perhaps, even rational and credible. As a mystery of faith, it is not something that reason can solve empirically or arrive at logically. In the end, only the light of divine grace can remove whatever doubts we might have regarding it and lead it to embrace it as a fundamental truth upon which our lives, our very destiny, hinges.

There is also an element of irony in the mystery of the Incarnation. Adam and Eve's desire to be like God, which they sought so selfishly in their primal fall from grace, happened to be in God's mind from the very outset. Their desire to be like God would have been bestowed on them freely by God himself had they not tried to go beyond their means and seize it by their own power for themselves. Theologians have debated for centuries whether the Incarnation would have taken place even if our first parents had never sinned. In one sense, this is a moot point, since we live in the reality of a fallen world and Christ is depicted as the New Adam, "the firstborn of all creation" (Col 1:15). In another sense, however, it is a very viable question, since it points out that God's love for humanity is not contingent on our flawed existence, but that his bounteous love for all human beings would ultimately bring him to our world so that he could lead us in friendship to our heavenly home.

An important flip side to the mystery of the Incarnation also comes to the forefront. God did not merely enter our world and become one of us. He did so that we might also enter his world and become divine like him. God has a plan for humanity, and was willing to go to great lengths to see it through. With our primal fall from grace leaving us helplessly lost and incapable of finding our way back home, God himself decided to reach down from heaven and enter our finite world to save and elevate us and make us like himself. His doing so changed the course of human history. Because of Jesus Christ, everyone who believes in him is an adopted son and daughter of the Father. His incarnation involved a movement of divine self-emptying, a process of *kenosis*, that Saint Paul so eloquently describes in his letter to the Philippians, saying that Christ, "though he was in the form of God, did not regard equality with God as something to be exploited, but emptied himself, taking the form of a slave, being born in human likeness" (Phil 2:5–7). In the end, the mystery of the Incarnation is all about the divine humility. Given the reality of humanity's fall from grace, God humbled himself that we might be exalted through our union with Christ's glorified and risen existence.

Reflection Questions

- Why do many people have such a difficult time accepting the Incarnation?

- What obstacles prevent them from accepting it?

- Do you have any such difficulties?

- What does this mystery say about God?

- What does it say about the world?

- What does it say about God's relationship to us?

Prayer

Lord, you entered our world and dwelled among us.

Help us to sense your presence in our midst and within our hearts.

3

Hanging from a Cross

CHRIST'S PASSION AND DEATH

> When it was noon, darkness came over the whole and until three in the afternoon. At three o'clock Jesus cried out with a loud voice, "Eloi, Eloi, lema sabachthani?" which means, "My God, my God, why have you forsaken me?" (Mark 15:33–34)

CHRISTIANS BELIEVE THAT GOD not only entered our world and became one of us, but that he also gave himself to us completely, to the point of dying for us. The relationship between the mysteries of Christ's incarnation and his passion and death appears in the opening verses of the New Testament, when the angel Gabriel tells Mary that her son will be called, "Emmanuel, which means, God is with us" (Matt 1:23). This title says that God entered our world to share in our lives and be with us. It reminds us that Jesus "was like us in all things, but sin" (Heb 4:15). The connection between the two mysteries also appears in Eastern Christian iconography of the Nativity of Our Lord, where artists often depict the swaddling clothes of the newborn babe and the dark cave into which he was born as foreshadowings of his tomb and burial wrappings.

Jesus, Christians believe, experienced all the joys of life, as well as all of its sorrows. He knew what it meant to suffer. He endured hardship, heartache, and pain. He suffered sickness and disease. He underwent a painful death on a cross. Jesus, they believe, carried this cross for each of us. The wounds of his passion represent every conceivable type of suffering. He took this suffering upon himself, freely and willingly, out of love for us. He also took our sins upon himself and paid the ultimate price for them: death. Jesus did all of this out of love for us. He entered our world to dwell among us, but also to suffer and die for us. Let us look more closely at the Jesus' passion and death, and let us begin by asking the following question: "Why?"

Why Did Jesus Suffer and Die?

Over the years, theologians have developed three theories to explain why Jesus of Nazareth suffered and died on the cross almost two thousand years ago: ransom, satisfaction, and moral instruction.[1]

The ransom theory developed within the patristic tradition and was prevalent for the first thousand years of the church's history. Evident in such thinkers as Augustine and Gregory the Great, it focuses on Jesus' saying that he came "to give his life as a ransom for many" (Matt 20:28). Jesus' death is understood as the ransom that God pays to Satan in order to release humanity from the chains of sin and death. This approach employs mythic language and sees Redemption as taking place on a cosmic plane in some grand battle between the forces of Christ and those of Satan. We are nothing but passive onlookers.

The satisfaction theory, in contrast, arose in the late eleventh-century work, the *Cur Deus homo* ("Why God Became Man"), by Anselm of Canterbury. It rejects the model of divine ransom and focuses instead on the infinite magnitude of the sin of Adam. This theory takes Satan completely out of the picture. Jesus, the expression of God's infinite compassion, dies on the cross, not to ransom us from Satan, but to satisfy the infinite demands of God's justice. Employing legal language, this theory eventually becomes the mainstay of church teaching and remains

---

1. See Billy, *Even Today*, 79–84.

so right up to the present. It puts humanity and God face to face. Jesus' death on the cross is understood as the way in which God's mercy satisfies the demands of God's justice. The wrath of God is quieted by his incarnate mercy.

The moral instruction theory rejected both the ransom and satisfaction models. First developed by the scholastic theologian Peter Abelard and adopted centuries later by a number of the proponents of Protestant liberalism, it insists that Jesus died on the cross not to ransom us from Satan or to satisfy God's justice, but to give us an example, that is, to show us how to love. It uses a variety of poetic images to convey the idea that Jesus' death on the cross reveals to those who experience it the true meaning of love. Jesus' humble act of total self-surrendering love is meant to move us and evoke from us a similar response.[2]

Unfortunately, these theories have not weathered time very well. They no longer speak to the heart. Perhaps they never did. They have become brittle and stale. Today they may be intellectually pleasing to an historian who studies the rise and interplay of ideas through time but, for the most part, they have lost their emotive force—they no longer inspire or move the heart. As the saying goes, "They are nothing to die for." One author puts the matter this way:

> Why should forgiveness require the shedding of blood?
> . . . Indeed, it is a question that has never been satisfactorily answered. To call the crucifixion a substitute punishment, or a sacrificial death, or a ransom, is merely to raise additional questions. Why would a good and gracious God require an innocent man to suffer and die for the forgiveness of others? Why would he demand a sacrifice? Why a lethal ransom? . . . And as far as satisfaction goes, how can God persuade sinners to rely on his merciful love when, all the while, they are enduring the awful consequences of his wrath. . . . None of these themes has explained to the satisfaction of modern people why

2. For an analysis of these various theories of redemption, see Aulén, *Christus Victor*, 143–59.

a death was necessary in God's scheme of things for our
sins to be forgiven.[3]

Why did Jesus have to die? Ransom? Satisfaction? To give us good
example? None of these explanations really give a satisfactory answer. They fail to convince us. We know instinctively that his death
could have been avoided and that Jesus' real reason for dying is
mysteriously hidden in the mind of God, our Father. In the words
of Alphonsus de Liguori, doctor of the church and patron of con-
fessors and moral theologians:

> It was not necessary for the Redeemer to die in order
> to save the world; a drop of his blood, a single tear, or
> prayer, was sufficient to procure salvation for all; for such
> a prayer, being of infinite value, should be sufficient to
> save not one but a thousand worlds.[4]

To understand the mystery of Christ and his cross, we must begin
to ask questions that come not from the head, but the heart. Once
we start doing that, we will find that the focus on Christ and his
cross will shift from a concentration on sin and satisfaction and be
understood more and more in light of God's response to human
suffering. Frances Young puts it this way:

> It is only because I can see God entering the darkness of
> human suffering and evil in his creation, recognizing it
> for what it really is, meeting it and conquering it, that I
> can accept a religious view of the world. Without the reli-
> gious dimension, life would be senseless, and endurance
> of its cruelty pointless; yet without the cross it would be
> impossible to believe in God.[5]

In a similar vein, Nikos Kazantzakis, in his quasi-autobiographical
novel *Report to Greco*, the last book written before his death in
1957, captures this contemporary experience of Christ and his
cross very well. He writes:

---

3. Anderson, "Why Was Christ's Death Necessary?" 19.

4. de Liguori, *Dignity and Duties of the Priest*, 26.

5. Leech, *Experiencing God*, 299-300.

In order to mount to the Cross, the summit of sacrifice, and to God, the summit of the Spirit, Christ passed through all the stages which the man who struggle passes through. All—and that is why his suffering is so familiar to us; that is why we pity Him, and why his final victory seems to us so much our own future victory. That part of Christ's nature which was profoundly human helps us to understand him and to love him and to pursue his passion as though it were our own. If he had not within him this warm human element, he would never be able to touch our hearts with such assurance and tenderness; He would not be able to become a model for our lives. We struggle, we see him struggle also, and we find strength. We see that we are not all alone in the world. He is fighting on our side.[6]

Why did Christ have to suffer and die? The answer will be very different depending upon whether these questions come from our head or our heart. Christ may have died to ransom us from the power of Satan, or to satisfy God's justice for Adam's sin, or to teach us the ways of virtue. He may have come for some mysterious combination of all of these things, which we cannot fully understand, and which is entirely known to the mind of God alone. After all is said and done, it may well be that he came simply to be with us—to be beside us as we struggle, to suffer as we suffer, to carry the cross that we ourselves will one day hang from. Jesus has gone before us. He has gone through it all and is right now beside us. This may not be very satisfactory intellectually. There is no overarching theory that makes sense out of everything. It leaves a lot of questions unanswered. It too fails to satisfy the mind, but it makes perfect sense to the heart—and to anyone who has ever been in love. Bushnell said, "There is a cross in God before the wood is seen on Calvary."[7] Christ's passion and death is God's response to our human suffering. Through it, God meets us where we are and knows that deep down inside all we really need to know is that we are loved.

6. Kazantzakis, *Report to Greco*, 278.
7. Bushnell, *The Vicarious Sacrifice*, 35.

Did Jesus Die for Me?

Jesus did not suffer and die for humanity in the abstract, but for each of us. To believe in Jesus is to trust in him. It takes his words to heart and trusts that they will come to pass. As he says in the Gospel of John, "God so loved the world that he gave his only Son, so that everyone who believes in him may not perish but may have eternal life" (John 3:16). Trust in Jesus leads to eternal life. We do so both as a community and as individuals. He suffered and died not just for the sins of humanity, but for each person who ever lived and who ever will live. All he asks of us is to trust him, to believe in him, to embrace his message and make it our own.

Some of us may ask, "How is it possible for one man to love so many people with such intensity?" Although we will never fully understand how God relates to us as a people, let alone as individuals, our faith tells us that the human and the divine, the natural and the supernatural, man and God, are somehow inextricably linked in the person of Jesus Christ, the Word made flesh, the God-man, the New Adam. Christians believe that, in him, all of humanity— as a whole and as individuals—has been given a fresh start. By believing in him, we become incorporated into his body and are empowered by his Spirit to overcome our self-centeredness and destructive egos and reach out to others.

That seed of faith, which is planted in us at Baptism and nourished by the other sacraments—especially the Eucharist— opens up to the life of divine grace and holiness. Through Christ and in his Spirit we become adopted sons and daughters of Father. The Word was made flesh and dwelled among us so that God himself could dwell in our hearts. He wants our hearts to dwell in his heart, and he also wants these very same hearts to become temples of his Spirit. Remember the words of Alphonsus de Liguori: "The paradise of God, so to speak, is the heart of man."[8] God does not treat humanity in the abstract, but wishes to dwell in *every* human heart. He can do so because, as the infinite God, he is not bound by finite boundaries and can enter the realm of our creaturely

8. See Chapter 2 Footnote 3 above.

limitations. He is a God of surprises and of impossible things. He can accomplish in us what we cannot do for ourselves. He can open for us the road to friendship and make possible for us to commune with his Spirit.

Did Jesus die for *me*? The answer to this question is an un-equivocal "Yes!" He died for each and every person who ever lived and who ever will live. He would have done so had you been the only person in need of Redemption. He is the Good Shepherd who is willing to leave the ninety-nine in search of the one who is lost (Luke 15:1–7). He is the "Hound of Heaven," who pursues us with purpose and determination, even as we flee from him and lose ourselves in our aimless pursuit of selfish pleasure that is fueled by our unruly passions. The implications of his passion and death are vast. If Jesus suffered and died so that we might once again enter into God's friendship, then we are called to respond with a free, faithful, and reciprocal response of love.

If Jesus died for us, then we are called to live for him. We live for him by following him, by walking in his footsteps, by taking up our cross daily and following him. Living the moral life, the good life, is a way of giving witness to Christ. Doing so is rarely easy, because there are so many counter voices urging us to do otherwise. It is the cross that every follower of Christ is asked to bear. It involves a dying to self and a placing of the needs of others before one's own. It is a type of martyrdom. It involves an empty-ing of self that goes beyond our natural capacity to do what is good and right. For the most part, this dying-to-self goes beyond our natural powers. We are not capable of emptying ourselves in such a way unless we receive the help of God's grace. If we try to do so on our own, we will sooner or later fall short. We will fail in small and even in serious ways.

Jesus' suffering and death led to an opening up of the channels of grace, which had been blocked by humanity's primal fall from grace. Jesus died for us so that we might be empowered by his Spirit to live the moral life. The life of Christian discipleship is not meant to be a joyless effort of will that carries out seemingly impossible demands imposed from without, but a life lived in the Spirit, whose presence within us enables us to do what otherwise might seem impossible. Jesus does not want disgruntled disciples, but followers filled with Gospel joy. He died for us so that we might live for others—and it is his spirit who empowers us to do so. When we turn our lives over to Jesus, his Spirit living within us makes the impossible possible. The words in Matthew's Gospel ring true:

> Come to me, all you that are weary and are carrying heavy burdens, and I will give you rest. Take my yoke upon you, and earn from me; for I am gentle and humble in heart, and you will find rest for your souls. For my yoke is easy, and my burden is light. (Matt 11:28–30)

With Christ's Spirit living in us, the yoke of the cross becomes an easy burden to carry. It gives our hearts gentleness, humility, rest—and so very much more.

The mystery of Jesus' passion and death was an event that took place both in and out of time: it happened *in* time, yet by transcending it eventually found itself *out* of it. Extending through the corridors of history, it has had repercussions for every age, people, and nation. At that tragic moment on Golgotha some two thousand years ago, past, present, and future mingled with timelessness, as the eternal consecrated time itself, making it holy by transforming *Chronos* (measured time) to *Kairos* (sacred time). This transfiguration of time points to another event that would occur both in and out of time, an event that would not take place on a hill, but in a tomb that the disciples would find empty some three days after their Master's death.

The mystery of Jesus' passion and death extends beyond both time, and the historical Jesus himself. It reaches out to his followers, to those who share in his vision of a kingdom already present, yet still to come. Jesus' passion and death continues to this day in the body of believers: he suffers and dies in us, as he suffers for us, and with us. When seen in this light, martyrdom is not some extraneous occurrence within the body of believers, but lies at the very heart of the Gospel message and gives new meaning to the phrase, "Take up your cross and follow me." As Tertullian once noted, "The blood of the martyrs is the seed of the Christians."[9] Being willing to give one's life for Christ is something all Christians must aspire to. Although few are called to it, and no one should actively seek it out, all must take up the yoke of the cross and give witness to Christ in their daily actions. The cross, we might say, is the tree of life, and the body of believers hangs from it to this very day.

Conclusion

What relevance does the mystery of Jesus' Passion and Death have for our daily lives? In the Gospel of John, Jesus tells his disciples, "This is my commandment, that you love one another as I have loved you" (John 15:12). He continues this thought by saying, "No one has greater love than this, to lay down one's life for one's friends" (John 15:13). He then concludes with, "You are my friends if you do what I command you" (John 15:14). It would be difficult to find a better summary of the relevance of the cross.

These three verses offer an excellent summary of Jesus' message to his disciples: he gives them a new commandment based on the love he has shown them; he then tells them that laying down one's life for one's friends is the greatest expression of love possible; and he finishes by saying that those who wish to befriend him do so by keeping his commandment of love. Jesus' conclusion is clear. His friends are called to love as he loved. If he gave of himself completely to the point of dying for others, then they are called to do the same.

In the mystery of his passion and death, Jesus showed us the greatest expression of death possible. When he tells his followers to take up their cross daily and follow him, he is telling them that they must go and do likewise. All are called to give witness to our faith in Christ. Like him, some of us may be asked to make the ultimate sacrifice. Others of us may be imprisoned or treated harshly by others on account of our faith. For most of us, however, the cross of Christ means living and loving for others by means of our daily

9. *Catechism of the Catholic Church*, no. 852.

actions. Scripture offers us certain guidelines for following him: the ten commandments, the gifts and fruits of the Spirit, the beatitudes. The creator of all things has also written a natural law in our hearts. If Scripture and natural law send us in the right direction, the passion and death of Jesus Christ gives us the clearest and most concrete example of what it means to love. When we look to the cross, we see the embodiment of God's love for humanity and all creation. By dying on the cross, God himself embraced the ravages of hatred, persecution, ridicule, physical and mental anguish, and death with love in his heart and forgiveness on his lips. If Jesus' self-emptying came to its climax in his passion and death, then its triumph came in the power of God's love manifested itself three days later in the empty tomb. Our hope in Jesus leads to our hope in the resurrection, both his and ours. Jesus' passion and death are not the end of his story or our own. Much more remains to be told.

Reflection Questions

- What do Jesus' suffering and death have to do with the mystery of redemption?
- Did Jesus have to suffer death in order to defeat it?
- If not, then why did God allow his Son to be humiliated in such a way?
- When you stand before a crucifix, what do you see?
- What do you want to see?
- What does God see?

Prayer

Lord, you suffered and died for us.

Help us to live for those around us.

4

"He Is Risen!"

The Empty Tomb

> But the angel said to the women, "Do not be afraid; I know that you are looking for Jesus who was crucified. He is not here; for he has been raised, as he said. Come, see the place where he lay. Then go quickly and tell his disciples, 'He has been raised from the dead, and indeed he is going ahead of you to Galilee; there you will see him.'" (Matt 28:5–7)

CHRISTIANITY WOULD NOT EXIST without the discovery of the empty tomb and the disciples' experience of the Risen Lord. The Easter proclamation, "He is risen!" lies at the very heart of the Christian message. Without it, there would be no Good News, nothing for us go out and announce to the world. The simple truth of the matter is that Jesus' resurrection from the dead either *did* or *did not* happen. As Christians, we stake our lives on it having happened to Jesus and, by placing our faith in him, hope one day to experience it for ourselves. If it did not occur, then the Apostle Paul's words apply to believers everywhere: "if Christ has not been raised, then our proclamation has been in vain and your faith has been in vain" (1 Cor 15:14). Let us explore both the idea of and our faith in the resurrection in more detail.

Thinking about Resurrection

Christians believe that, at some point after death, a follower of Christ is transformed by the power of the God on every level of his or her human makeup—the physical, the mental, the spiritual, and the communal—and thus raised to a higher level of human existence in a way that always remains in fundamental continuity with his or her historical, earthly life. For us, resurrection means personal life after death in a transformed state that embraces all aspects of human existence in a way continuous with a person's concrete, earthly life.

This description sets resurrection apart from the related idea of bodily resuscitation such as the raising of Lazarus (John 11:44), as well as from the other major philosophical and religious explanations of the nature of life in the hereafter. Resurrection distinguishes itself from bodily resuscitation in its emphasis on a transformed existence in life after death. It differs from the immortality of the soul in its inclusion of all of humanity's anthropological factors in the nature of that existence. It is distinguished from reincarnation in its rupture of the cycle of time and its insistence on the fundamental continuity of life in the hereafter with a person's earthly existence. It breaks with Nirvana in its avowal that final beatitude does not involve the extinction of individual consciousness.

Of all of the notions about the nature of life after death, resurrection alone safeguards the inviolate dignity of each human being on every level of his or her existence. As an idea, its greatest strength is that it alone keeps human nature eternally intact while, at the same time, saving the individual from ultimate personal extinction. Its greatest weakness is that, in representing the fulfillment of one of the deepest and most profound hopes of the human heart, it seems almost too good to be true, an attractive, yet highly unlikely, possibility. For this reason, of all the ideas of life in the hereafter, resurrection is the one most difficult to accept on the simple basis of faith.

On the Third Day

Rooted in the hopes of Jewish apocalypticism during the centuries just prior to the appearance of Christ, and promulgated during Jesus' own lifetime by the devout religious group known as the Pharisees, the idea of resurrection developed to its present form as a result of theological reflection on the nature of Christ's paschal mystery, most especially in the primitive Christian community's interpretation of the meaning of the apostolic experience of the Risen Lord. This reflection is intimately tied to the trust that community placed in the validity of the apostolic witness and to the experience of faith upon which it rested. It is also the context within which one may speak of the resurrection not merely as an idea, but as a reality and a hope.

What precisely happened on that first Easter morning, three days after Jesus' suffering and death on Golgotha, remains shrouded by the mysterious character of the event itself and by the subjective awareness of the earliest followers of Jesus. That awareness probably ran the gamut of several emotional states—from depression and fear, to suspicion and isolation, to incipient faith and the lingering yearning for the retrieval of lost expectations—and most likely varied in each of the persons involved. That is not to say that the event has no basis outside the experience of Jesus' followers, but only that there is no way to determine what it is with any historical accuracy. The Easter event, in other words, touches history, but extends far beyond it. Probably the most important consequence of this unique encounter is the faith experience of Jesus' immediate followers that provided the original impetus for the rise and spread of the earliest Christian communities. The faith of the church universal rests upon the foundation of these earliest apostolic witnesses.

At this point, we need to distinguish between the faith of those who witnessed the Easter event personally and those whose faith relies on the testimony of the apostles. The proclamation of the church rests upon the eyewitness accounts of the apostles, that is, on those who made the startling claim to have experienced for themselves the reality of the Risen Lord. Their experience of faith remains qualitatively different from that of the believer in the pew, for they claim to have experienced a reality outside of themselves, rooted in the objective order, distinct from their own subjectivity, and identified with the person of their master, Jesus of Nazareth. Without the unprecedented boldness and resiliency of these claims, the Christian project would have nothing distinctive in its message and possibly might never have gotten off the ground.

These apostolic claims emerge from one of two possibilities: the experience of the Risen Christ was either *with* or *without* a basis in the person of Jesus in the external, objective order. That is to say, the experience of the apostles either corresponds to a reality outside of themselves or remains entirely subjective in all respects. If the former is true, then the further question must be asked regarding the nature of this basis in the external order. If the latter were true, then the only conclusion to be drawn is that the apostles suffered from self-delusion, that their testimony is false, as is the religion to which it gave rise. The fact that neither of these possibilities can be proven highlights the underlying quality of faith inherent in the conclusions of both the believer and non-believer alike.

Still more can be said about the position of the believer. If the apostolic experience of the Risen Christ *does* have an external basis in the person of Jesus, then this affirmation, when combined with the idea of resurrection developed earlier, necessarily points to an event of singular historical significance; indeed, an event which could be measured by the instruments of historical observation only by its effects (for example, a missing body) and which, for this reason, must be placed in a category unique to itself and understood as a transhistorical event with historical consequences. This is so precisely because the Risen Christ, existing in a transformed state but in a way continuous with his earthly life, does not lead a "historical existence" in the way in which the phrase is commonly used. That is to say that space and time no longer set the limits for his physical existence. In his resurrected state, Christ is the Alpha and the Omega, a singular dimension unique unto himself, who recapitulates, both now and forever, all of Creation within himself, into the love of the Father and the joy of their Spirit.

In its essence, belief in the resurrection consists in the affirmation that the idea of resurrection has become a reality in the Risen Christ. This reality is rooted in the transhistorical nature of Christ's paschal mystery, the historical consequences of which linger even to this day in the ongoing proclamation of the church. Based on the testimony of its apostolic forebears, the church has, in its ministry down through the centuries, kept alive for humanity the fervent hope that the deepest yearnings of the human heart will one day be fully realized. That is to say that the transformation wrought by God in Christ promises to extend itself to all who are incorporated into his body, the church. In this respect, a sharing in the life of the Risen Lord may be looked upon as the ultimate destiny of all of humankind and will be impeded only by a stubborn private or corporate persistence in the life of sin.

Some Implications

To affirm that the idea of resurrection has become a reality is to utilize the well-known distinction between the subjective and objective orders. While, this distinction is not without its limitations, and while care must be taken not to stretch the analogy beyond its avowed usefulness, it allows us to examination some of the implications of the Christian belief in the resurrection.

To begin with, Christians believe that God the Father is the primary agent in bringing about this realization in Christ. Since idea and reality are intimately connected in God's vision of himself, the resurrection of Christ may be viewed as a providential movement on the part of the Father to bring his plan of redemption in accord with the working of the Divine Mind. In this respect, Christ's resurrection is that event which, touching upon history but transcending time, initiates the ultimate return of all created things back to God. Similarly, this view of Christ's resurrection sheds light upon the development in the early church of the doctrine of the Incarnation. If, in Christ's resurrection, flesh has been divinized and lifted up into the reality of the Word, it is easy to see how early Christians would come to believe that, at some point prior to this momentous occasion, the Word itself had descended into the reality of human flesh and become human. Putting aside for the moment, the various intricacies involved in discussing the christological controversies in the early centuries of the church, it seems quite appropriate to say that the doctrines of Christ's incarnation and resurrection form two aspects of a single salvific event. Christ's resurrection, in other words, is not merely the state of Christ's postmortem existence, but an intimate part of the whole process of redemption. If Christ's redemptive mission reaches its furthest extension in his passion and death on the cross, then his return to the Father is ushered in by the events of Easter morning, and his Spirit is the principle by which all things continue to be gathered into his body and thus into the presence of the Father. It is in this sense that all things are recapitulated in Christ, the New Adam (Rom 5:15).

Moreover, as a transhistorical event with historical consequences, the resurrection of Christ exists outside of but in relation to the realm of historical inquiry. In this regard, it lies beyond the realm of scientific investigation and can be affirmed only through faith in the testimony of those claiming to have actually experienced Jesus after his death. That is not to say that the apostles did not experience something outside of themselves (i.e., in the external order), but only that the basis for their experience cannot be verified. Indeed, probably the only historical consequence of measurable scientific value would have been the disappearance of Jesus' body at the actual moment of his resurrection. Since the precise whereabouts of the body was a point of contention even in the initial aftermath of the Easter proclamation (Matt 28:13), one must conclude that, although its disappearance at this time could have been verified, if not scientifically, then at least through impartial eyewitness accounts, it obviously was not.

On all other points, a detached observer may not have been able to separate the subjective experience of the apostles from the reality of the Risen Christ. In other words, there may have been no way of determining whether or not they were actually experiencing anything beyond their own intensified inner awareness. The singularity of this experience would be expected if a transhistorical event were to occur and be experienced in its historical consequences. To the extent that it is not based on direct experience but on the testimony of others, the faith of subsequent Christian believers is qualitatively different from the faith of the apostles. Not only does it rest on the conviction of those who claimed to have had an actual experience of the Risen Lord, but, in one respect, it is even a purer experience of faith: "Blessed are those who have not seen and yet have believed" (John 20:29).

Finally, belief in the Risen Christ keeps alive in people the hope that, after death, their lives will not end, but merely be changed. Because of Christ's resurrection, they look forward to a transformed existence in the hereafter, one in continuity with their lives on earth. Sustained by a believer's prayerful response to the contemporary challenges of Christian discipleship, this hope forms the basis upon which life in the resurrection is anticipated even in the present. Through their participation in the ministry and life of the church, people receive a foretaste of this transformed existence, especially when they partake of the sacraments around the table of the Lord. At Emmaus, Jesus' disciples recognized him in the breaking of the bread (Luke 24:30). Today, Christians seek the same when they gather in churches throughout the world to celebrate the Eucharist.[1]

Proclaiming the Resurrection

The truth of the Christian message hinges on the belief that Jesus emerged from the empty tomb alive. Every aspect of the human Jesus—physical, mental, spiritual, communal—was transformed and glorified, "divinized" if you will. Although a deep change took place, there was still a fundamental continuity between his historical and risen existences. This transformation took place

1. See Billy, "The Resurrection Kernel," 206–16.

because of the Father's love for the Son, and showed that the bond between them was greater than even death itself. When seen in this light, Jesus' resurrection is intimately related to the mystery of divine love. If "God is love" (1 John 4:8), then Jesus hanging from the cross embodies it, and his resurrection from the dead demonstrates its power.

The Gospel proclaims Jesus' resurrection as the first fruit of the new creation. Both the Son of God and Son of Man, he took on our humanity so that we might share in his divinity. His passion, death, and resurrection allowed this to take place, and our destiny is now forever intertwined with his. Christ's paschal mystery has changed everything. God's love for us is overwhelming. We stand before the cross in sorrow, and stare into the empty tomb with renewed hope. We live in hope, because we believe that what happened to Jesus will one day happen to all who look to him in faith. The words of the Apostle Paul ring true: "He will transform the body of our humiliation that it may be conformed to the body of his glory, by the power that also enables him to make all things subject to himself" (Phil 3:21).

Jesus' resurrection dispels the darkness of sin and death and proclaims the dawn of a new era. For now, his glorified existence is hidden in the hearts of his followers. We proclaim his message not only with our words, but also with our actions. Every time we act in love, we give flesh to our belief in the resurrection. Every gesture of kindness is an assertion of faith and a proclamation of hope. Jesus himself told his disciples to go throughout the word and make disciples of all nations. The purpose of this apostolic mission is to proclaim the reality of Christ's resurrection and the power of God's love. The message we proclaim is one of power and glory. Nothing more, nothing less. "Christ has died. Christ has risen. Christ will come again." It is also a message of humility and compassion, one that finds love, not chaos, at the heart of reality. It sees history slowly drawing to a close and all things being swept up by the merciful embrace of the Glorified and Risen Lord.

We live in an in-between time, with Jesus' first coming already passed and his second yet to come. Our task during this interim period is to proclaim the good news of Christ's Resurrection. We do this to help others recognize their inborn dignity as human beings created in God's image and kindle in them the hope that, tarnished though it may be, this image can be made to reflect the light of God's love in a way never before thought possible. God's love is transforming. The proclamation of Jesus' resurrection from the dead reminds us that this transforming power extends to every dimension of our human makeup—physical, mental, spiritual, and communal—indeed, to all of creation. Jesus' resurrection represents the first fruit of the new creation: "See, I am making all things new" (Rev 21:5).

Conclusion

Jesus' resurrection represents the birth of a new, recreated humanity. All of us have the opportunity to share in this new creation. To do so, we need to look to Jesus, allow him to befriend us, and invite him to live in our hearts. This mutual indwelling of Jesus in us and us in him occurs in the depths of the soul, what the Apostle Paul calls the "spirit" (1 Thess 5:23). It is there where the Spirit of Jesus communes with us and gives us a spirit of adoption: "When we cry. 'Abba! Father!' it is that very Spirit bearing witness with our spirit that we are children of God, and if children, then heirs, heirs of God and joint heirs with Christ—if, in fact, we suffer with him so that we may also be glorified with him" (Rom 8:15–17).

We must not overlook this connection between suffering and glory. Jesus' resurrection would not have happened without his passion and death. Those were a necessary prelude to his elevation and splendor. The same holds true for us. As adopted sons and daughters of the Father, our lives are now intimately bound up with his Son's. Jesus continues to live his paschal mystery through us, the members of his body. His passion, death, and resurrection provide the underlying pattern according to which we ourselves are shaped. Because of him, our suffering and deaths are now intimately bound up with his. His rising from the dead, in turn, represents a glorified, transformed existence that we hope to share and, to some extent, already sense. Because of Jesus' resurrection, we are able to clothe ourselves with the new self, "created according to the likeness of God in true righteousness and holiness" (Eph 4:24).

Central as it may be to the Christian narrative, Jesus' resurrection remains but a single aspect of the Father's salvific plan for humanity. The narrative of redemption continues. Although everything leads up to and flows from Jesus' resurrection, his mission is not complete until he returns to the Father. The gospels tell us that Jesus appeared to his disciples several times during the forty days after his resurrection and then ascended into heaven to sit in glory at the right hand of the Father. Only then could he send his Spirit to his followers to empower them to follow, to take up the cross of the gospel and follow in his path.

Reflection Questions

- What does Jesus' resurrection tell us about life?
- What does it tell us about death?
- What does it tell us about God's power?
- What does it tell us about God's love for us?
- What does it say about God's plan for us?
- What does it say about God's plan for you?

Prayer

Lord, you gave us the empty tomb.

Help us to empty our hearts for your risen glory.

5

He Was Lifted Up

The Ascension

> Jesus said to her, "Do not hold on to me, because I have not
> yet ascended to the Father. But go to my brothers and say to
> them, 'I am ascending to my Father and your Father, to my
> God and your God.'" (John 20:17)

JESUS CAME FROM THE Father and was destined to return to him.
This was part of the Father's plan from the very outset. He sent
his Son to enter our world, live among us, and die for us. Jesus'
willingness to empty himself in this way demonstrates his love
for the Father and the extent to which he was willing to go to save
us from the powers of darkness. Jesus desired only to do the Father's will. This determination led him to Golgotha, to the empty
tomb, and (some forty days after his resurrection) to his glorious
and triumphant return to the Father. The Father raised his Son
to draw him back to himself. In his return, Jesus, the God-man,
brought our humanity back with him. The mystery of his ascension, we might say, represents the completion of Jesus' redemptive journey. Once at his Father's side, he was free to impart his
Spirit to those he left behind.

The Beginning of the End

We can best understand the significance of Jesus' ascension by viewing it against the backdrop of the Incarnation and paschal mystery. All of the mysteries of redemption are intimately related, and this is especially true for the closing act of the drama of Christ's redemptive mission.

Although it is true that the Blessed Trinity always acts as one, individual aspects of God's providential activity in the world have typically been associated with one specific person. The mystery of creation is associated with the Father; that of redemption, with the Son; that of sanctification, with the Holy Spirit. The ascension represents the final moment of Christ's redemptive journey, after which time the sanctifying work of the Spirit would begin. It is the final act in the drama of Christ's activity in the world. This work has a beginning, middle, and end: he who came from the Father must one day return to him. The underlying principle that underlies all of Christ's redemptive activity—that God became human so that humanity might become divine—helps us to place this mystery in the context of the other mysteries of the Redemption. God became human in the mystery of the Incarnation. He saved us from the powers of darkness in the mystery of his passion, death, and resurrection. He divinizes our humanity by bringing our human nature with him in his ascension to the right hand of the Father.

In some respects, the ascension represents the end of one story and the beginning of another. On the one hand, it is the end of Christ's work of redemption, which was needed because of humanity's primal fall from grace, without which there would not be a need for Christ to come into the world and do for us what we could not do for ourselves. Without the fall, there would have been no need for the incarnation of God's Son, no need for his suffering and death, no need for his resurrection and ascension into heaven. With his return in glory to the Father, Jesus has completed the work of redemption, and the work of the Spirit can begin.

On the other hand, the ascension makes possible the beginning of the Spirit's sanctifying mission in and through the members of Christ's body, the church. If Christ's ascension marks the end of the work of redemption, it also makes possible the first moments of humanity's sanctification. As Jesus himself says in the Gospel of John: "[I]t is to your advantage that I go away, for if I do not go away, the Advocate will not come to you; but if I go, I will send him to you" (John 16:7). With Christ's ascension, human nature has been healed and elevated to a new level. Christ's redemptive work, however, must now be applied to each individual by the work of the Holy Spirit (acting through various means, but primarily through the church and her sacraments).

Rising from the Fall

Let us take a closer look at the ascension's relationship to the other mysteries of the faith, and let us begin by looking at its relationship to the fall. At first, the ascension may seem to have little to do with humanity's primal fall from grace. One occurs at the dawn of human history; the other, at the end of Christ's redemptive activity on earth. One brings to light the self-destructive disintegrating pull of evil, while the other represents God's glorification of his beloved Son. One has to do with the ramifications of sin and death; the other, with the elevation of the one who has defeated them.

On another level, however, the two mysteries complement one another and actually go hand in hand. If the fall symbolizes fallen humanity, then the ascension represents an anticipation of a fully redeemed humanity. The ascension, in other words, announces the complete and utter reversal of the fall. In the mystery of our primal fall from grace, human nature suffered a serious weakening of all of its powers. Our minds became darkened; our wills weakened; our passions unruly. What is more, our bodies grew out of sync with our souls, our spirits lost touch with God, and our communal consciousness became fragmented. Christ's ascension, by way of contrast, represents the return of the glorified Christ, in both his humanity and his divinity, to the right hand of the Father. Through Jesus and because of him, humanity could enter the presence of the Father and share in Christ's sonship. The ascension shows us where we belong. It marks our place in the vast scheme of the new creation: to sit with Christ at the Father's side. That is precisely why the Apostle tells us we are now God's children, adopted sons and daughters of the Father (see Eph 1:5).

Christ's ascension represents the divine counterweight to Adam's fall, an action of divinity to right the primal wrongs of sinful humanity. Jesus' return to the Father marks humanity's entrance into the kingdom of light. As a result of Christ's redemptive mission, human nature was not merely healed, but elevated. If, prior to the fall, humanity enjoyed the fellowship of God, then after the ascension it shared in the intimacy of the divine sonship. Because of it, our darkened minds were enlightened beyond all telling; our weakened wills were strengthened and uplifted; our passions became ordered and made holy; our communal self-awareness was regained and deepened by our participation in the intimate love of the Trinity. Christ's ascension allows humanity to enter the presence of the Father. Jesus said he would show us the way to the Father, and he would make good on his promise. He was a trailblazer who cleared a way for us and showed us the path to follow. We can walk this path only with him as our guide, since only he can return to the Father.

Rising from the Dead

If the ascension represents the ultimate reversal of the fall, then Christ's passion, death, and resurrection were the means by which it took place. They are the heart of Christ's redemptive activity; his ascension, its dramatic dénouement. Some may wish to see Christ's resurrection and ascension as two sides of the same coin, and in a sense they are. Taken together, they represent divinity's foil to the corruption of sin. Jesus' resurrection, preceded as it was by his passion and death, signals the defeat of sin and death. On account of it, the devil's stranglehold over fallen humanity was broken, and we were set free to pursue God's plan for our lives.

The ascension takes this defeat of death one step further. It represents more than merely overcoming death and entering into an elevated state of existence. It recognizes that the proper place for this new creation, this glorified and divinized humanity made possible by the resurrection, is not this present earthly existence, but next to the Father's right hand. Jesus was "lifted up" not only from the grave, but also from this earthy existence. He did so while bringing his transformed material existence with him to a new heaven and a new earth. The old order of things has passed away; Christ came to make all things new (Rev 21:45).

The ascension brings the dramatic action of Christ's resurrection to its logical conclusion. Jesus rose from the dead to return to the Father and bring his humanity along with it. His redemptive action is made complete with his return to the Father. Sitting at the Father's right hand, he reigns over the universe (indeed, over all reality) as Pantocrator, King of Kings, and Prince of Peace. From there, he rules over the entire universe and wishes to reign in our hearts as our Loving, Just, and Merciful Lord. To accomplish this task, he sends his Spirit to move us to open our hearts to his love. His ascent to the Father makes the descent of the Spirit possible. Through this mystery, we are empowered to share in every aspect of Christ's saving action.

Rising in the Spirit

The aftermath of Jesus' ascension into heaven is life in the Spirit and the quest for holiness. In order to complete his messianic mission, the Risen and Glorified Lord had to return to the Father's side. Once there, he poured out his Spirit upon the earth and ignited a divine romance of the human heart. This love affair with humanity takes place in the depths of each and every soul. It begins with a fundamental principal: "Do good and avoid evil." From there, it reaches outward to embrace the desire to live, share in family, and promote peace and justice and to live in harmony. Ultimately, it seeks to live in God and for God. This "natural law" represents the remnant of God's image remaining in the human heart after the Fall. It has been thoroughly transformed by virtue of Christ's passion, death, resurrection, and ascension into heaven. Jesus' return to the Father, in other words, changes everything. From now on we have a New Law to contend with. It is the Law of the New Covenant, the love of the Spirit, the law of God's love, the law of the new creation, the law of the new humanity.

The New Testament does not offer a clear picture of exactly what happened at Jesus' ascension into heaven and the subsequent gift of the Spirit. Matthew's Gospel says only that the Risen Lord appeared to the Eleven on a mountain in Galilee, where he told them to make disciples of all nations, to baptize in the name of the Father, Son, and Spirit, and to remember that he will be with them always (Matt 28:16–20). Mark's Gospel makes no mention of the Spirit, but simply states that the Risen Lord appeared to the Eleven when they were at table and instructed them to proclaim the good news to all creation, after which time he was taken up into heaven to sit at the right hand of God (Mark 16:14–20). John's Gospel refers to Jesus "return to the Father" (John 20:17) and describes in dramatic fashion his imparting of the Spirit to his disciples (John 20:22). Luke ends his Gospel with Jesus blessing his disciples at Bethany, withdrawing from them, and being carried up into heaven (Luke 24:50–51). In the Acts of the Apostles, Luke gives his readers some more details. Before returning to his proper place at his Father's side, Jesus promises his disciples to send them his Spirit to instruct them and guide them. He fulfills this promise some ten days later on the feast of Pentecost. The Spirit manifests himself to the disciples in a powerful wind and tongues of fire appearing over their heads to signify an overpowering love that took possession of their hearts, and empowering them to speak in foreign tongues, thus symbolizing the universal scope of the Gospel message (Acts 2:1–13). The various discrepancies in the accounts probably stem from a number of factors: the lack of empirical evidence, the variety of witnesses, the intent of the Gospel writers, and—perhaps most importantly—the transhistorical nature of Christ's paschal mystery. Despite these inconsistencies, they still convey a clear sense that the Gospel includes the proclamation that Jesus has risen from the dead, that he returned to the Father, and that he sent his Spirit to his disciples. Whether these events took place over an extended period of time or in a more integrated manner remains unclear.

One of the best ways of understanding the relationship between Jesus' return to the Father and the descent of the Holy Spirit can be found in Jesus' words to his disciples: "As the Father has sent me, so I send you" (John 20:21). There are two missions mentioned here: the redemptive mission of Jesus and the apostolic mission of his disciples. Each begins with a sending of the Holy Spirit. At the Annunciation, Mary conceived by the power of the Holy Spirit and eventually gave birth to Jesus, the Son of God (Luke 1:35). At the birth of the church on Pentecost, this same Spirit descended upon those gathered in the upper room (Acts 2:1–13). Interestingly enough, Jesus' mother, Mary, was present at each of these moments, giving continuity to the two missions and also implying that she was not only the mother of Jesus, but also the mother of the church (Acts 1:12–14). The parallel between Jesus' mission and the mission of his body, the church, continues. Jesus preaches and heals; the church proclaims God's Word and celebrates his healing and life-giving sacraments. Jesus suffers, dies, and rises to new life; the members of his body, the church, share in this paschal mystery by giving witness to the Gospel in their lives, sometimes to the point of death. Jesus' mission redeems; the church's mission is to sanctify by the power of the Holy Spirit. Jesus returns to the Father; the church, as the body of the Risen Lord, lives in history, yet yearns to reign with him. Mary, the mother of our Lord and the mother of the church, has, in fact, already joined him in the mystery of her assumption and reigns with him as queen of heaven. As Jesus' first and closest disciple, she has experienced the fullness of redemption and embodies the hope of all of Jesus' followers.

The redemptive mission of the Son continues in the sanctifying mission of the church, whose members are empowered by the presence of the Spirit in their lives. Christ's redemptive mission makes possible the apostolic mission of the church. The church gives witness to what the Second Vatican Council refers to as the "universal call to holiness."[1] That call is intimately linked to the

---

1. See Second Vatican Council, *Lumen Gentium*, nos. 39–42.

call to discipleship and the belief that God wills the salvation of all human beings. If the ascension marks the end of Christ's redemptive journey, it also sets the stage for the release of Christ's Spirit at Pentecost and the apostolic mission of the disciples. Just as each mission began with a descent of the Holy Spirit, so each one ends with a return to the Father. Jesus marks the end of his redemptive mission in this manner. The mission of his disciples has already begun in the mystery of Mary's assumption, and will draw to a close at the end of time when the dead shall be raised to life and face their final judgment. Until that time, the Holy Spirit continues to empower his followers to give witness to the Risen Lord by dedicating their lives to the spread of the Gospel. God's word has purpose and direction. It does not return in vain (Isa 55:11). Jesus, the Word of God made flesh, returned to the Father in his Risen Glory. The Word proceeding from the mouth of the church shall do the same.

Conclusion

The ascension is an integral part of the Gospel proclamation. It completes the narrative of Christ's redemptive journey by bringing him back to his Father's side, the place where it all began. Through it, one circle of God's providential plan closes and another opens. As the process of the divine self-emptying gives way to Jesus' glorification by the Father, another divine initiative— that of humanity's sanctification—begins. Jesus, in other words, does not return to the Father empty-handed. Having accomplished his redemptive mission, he brings back with him a divinized human nature that now makes it possible for each of us to share in his divine sonship. Jesus' ascension reminds us that the purpose of his redemptive mission was to make it possible for us to become adopted sons and daughters of the Father. With it, Jesus' work to free us from sin and death ends, and the sanctifying mission of the Spirit begins.

Jesus, the Eternal Word, was once called the "Eternal Child of the Father."[2] His return to the Father is a celebration of the Father's love for his Son and, indeed, for all of humanity. If we wish to accompany him at the Father's side, we must receive him like little children. We do so by opening our hearts to him and allowing his Spirit to dwell within us. His ascension makes this divine indwelling possible. Jesus entered our world to show us the way back to the Father. Doing so meant becoming one of us, living among us, suffering and dying for us, rising to new life, returning to the Father, and ultimately sending us his Spirit. His ascension marks the end of his redemptive journey and the beginning of our own journey of discipleship. We follow the discipline of our master by allowing his Spirit to dwell within us and gently transform us from within. Through the power of his Spirit, we hope to shed our prodigal ways and return to the loving embrace of a compassionate and merciful Father.

Jesus referred to himself as "the way, and the truth, and the life" (John 14:6). The mystery of the ascension affirms this fundamental truth of the Christian faith. His return to the Father anticipates our own journey home. Not returning to the Father would have cast doubt on the possibility of us joining him one day at his Father's side. Without the ascension, the path to truth and to fullness of life would be incomplete. This mystery completes the circle of Christ's redemptive journey. It affirms the Father's dream for humanity and reminds us that nothing can separate us from the love of God.

Reflection Questions

- How is Christ's ascension the end of one process and the beginning of another?

- How does it complete Christ's work of redemption?

- What process does it open up?

2. Balthasar, *A Theological Anthropology*, 257.

- What does it say about our place in God's providential plan?
- What does it mean for Jesus to sit at the right hand of the Father?
- Who else is with him?

Prayer

Lord, you completed your task and returned to the Father.

Help us to follow your Spirit and find our way home.

Conclusion

Jesus Christ is "making all things new" (Rev 21:5). His appearance on the world scene marks the beginning of a new creation. He came to free humanity from the stranglehold of sin and death, heal it of its wounds, and lift it to new heights. He is the light of the world that casts out the darkness from our souls and fills it with the warming flame of his Spirit. He is the culmination of salvation history, "the Alpha and the Omega, the first and the last, the beginning and the end" (Rev 22:13). He is the Redeemer, the Prince of Peace, King of Kings, Son of God and Son of Man. Before him every knee shall bend and every tongue proclaim to the glory of God the Father, "Jesus Christ is Lord" (Phil 2:10–11).

Jesus Christ is all of these things, and so very much more. He has special significance for us, because he is also the New Adam, the firstborn of the new creation, the father of the new humanity. He came from the Father on a mission to redeem the world and establish it anew. He accomplished this task by entering our world and living among us, by giving himself to us completely to the point of dying for us, by nourishing us with his own body and blood, and by becoming a source of hope for us. The mysteries of his incarnation, passion, death, resurrection, and ascension provide the narrative basis of his redemptive journey. Once he completed this mission, he would return to the Father's side in glory and, from that privileged place in heaven, send his Spirit to dwell in the hearts of the members of his body, the church, to begin a new task of making disciples of all nations, "baptizing them in the name of the Father and of the Son and of the Holy Spirit" (Matt 28:19).

This task of evangelizing and sanctifying the nations will go on until the end of time. It involves the preaching of the good news of Christ's resurrection and spells out its implications for all humanity. This task has been entrusted to his body, the church, and involves proclaiming the Word (*kerygma*), celebrating the sacraments (*liturgia*), and living in the service of charity (*diakonia*). It means serving others by seeking to fulfill the new commandment given to those who share in his new humanity: "Love one another. Just as I have loved you, you also should love one another" (John 13:34–35). We can live out this commandment only because the Spirit of Christ himself dwells in our hearts and helps us. This Spirit is our Advocate, our Helper, our Paraclete. He inspires us and prompts us to follow in the footsteps of Jesus. He accompanies us on our journey. He encourages and strengthens us. He blesses us with his manifold gifts and fruits. He enables us to take the message of the beatitudes to heart. He sanctifies us and guides us. He leads us back to the Risen Lord and reminds us of his parting words to his disciples, "Remember, I am with you always, to the end of the age" (Matt 28:20).

Lastly, as followers of Christ, we see in his mother, Mary, the fullness of everything we hope for. We see her as Jesus' first and closest disciple, who followed him throughout his earthly life, and beyond. She is full of grace, full of the Spirit, full of the love of God. She conceived by the power of the Holy Spirit and gave birth to the Savior of the world. Because of her humble *fiat* and her unique role in her God's plan for our salvation, she now possesses the fullness of redemption. Like Jesus, she too bears many titles. She is *Theotokos*, the God-bearer. She is Mother of God, Queen of Heaven, Queen of Peace, Mother of the Church, the Immaculate Conception, and countless others. If Jesus is the New Adam, then she is the New Eve, the Mother of the New Humanity. She is our Mother, always looking out for us, always interceding for us, always pleading to her Son on our behalf. Her only desire is to lead us to her Son; "To Jesus through Mary," as the saying goes. Jesus is the way, and she was the first to follow him. With Jesus, her Son, she wishes to reign in our hearts. Both she and her Son ask of us nothing more than for us to open our hearts to them and allow this to happen.

Bibliography

Anderson, W. William. "Why Was Christ's Death Necessary?" Harvard Divinity Bulletin 21/1 (1991–92) 18–22.

Aulén, Gustaf. Christus Victor: An Historical Analysis of the Three Main Types of the Idea of Atonement. Translated by A. G. Herbert. New York: Macmillan, 1969.

Balthasar, Hans Urs von. A Theological Anthropology. New York: Sheed and Ward, 1967.

Billy, Dennis J. Even Today: Theology and the Inner Child. Staten Island, NY: Alba, 1995.

————. "The Resurrection Kernel." Review for Religious 51 (1992) 206–16.

Bushnell, Horace. The Vicarious Sacrifice. London: Richard D. Dickinson, 1880.

Catechism of the Catholic Church. Vatican City: Libreria Editrice Vaticana, 1994.

de Liguori, Alphonsus. Dignity and Duties of the Priest, or Selva. The Complete Ascetical Works of St. Alphonsus de Liguori. Edited by Eugene Grimm. Vol. 12. Brooklyn, NY: Redemptorist Fathers, 1927.

————. The Way to Converse Always and Familiarly with God. Vol. 2, The Complete Ascetical Works of Alphonsus de Liguori. Edited by Eugene Grimm. Brooklyn, NY: Redemptorist Fathers, 1926.

Denzinger, Heinrich. Compendium of Creeds, Definitions, and Declarations on Matters of Faith and Morals. 43rd edition. Edited by Peter Hünermann for the original bilingual edition. Edited by Robert L. Fastiggi and Anne Englund Nash for the English edition. San Francisco: Ignatius, 2012.

Kazantzakis, Nikos. Report to Greco. Translated by P. A. Bien. New York: Simon and Schuster, 1965.

Leech, Kenneth. Experiencing God: Theology as Spirituality. San Francisco: Harper and Row, 1985.

Phillips, J. B. Your God Is Too Small. New York: Macmillan, 1967.

Second Vatican Council. Lumen Gentium. In Vatican Council II: The Conciliar and Post-Conciliar Documents. Edited by Austin Flannery. Collegeville, MN: Liturgical, 1992.

Made in the USA
Middletown, DE
01 February 2018